So You Want To

BUILD A CASTLE

Alex Woolf

Illustrated by George Bletsis,
Martin Bustamante and Will Morris

OXFORD
UNIVERSITY PRESS

CONTENTS

LET'S DESIGN YOUR CASTLE! 4

CASTLE BUILDING BASICS 5
   Location, Location, Location 5
   Parts of a Castle 6
   What Type of Castle Should You Choose? 8
   What Rooms Will You Have in Your Castle? 10
   What Will Life Be Like in Your Castle? 12

SPECIAL FEATURES FOR YOUR CASTLE 14
   Learning from the Best 14
   Design and Decoration 16

KEEPING OUT THE ENEMY 18
   Up Against the Wall 20

UNDER ATTACK 22
   Bombarding Your Castle 24
   A Fair Fight? 25

LEARNING FROM THE PAST 26
   The Siege of Castle Gaillard, 1203–04 27
   The Siege of Rochester Castle, 1215 31
   The Siege of Dover Castle, 1216–17 36
   The Siege of Kenilworth Castle, 1266 40

BUILDING YOUR CASTLE 50

GLOSSARY 54

INDEX 55

LET'S DESIGN YOUR CASTLE!

It's the late Middle Ages, the year is 1490 and Henry VII is the King of England. You are a **noble** who has recently been rewarded by the King and now you have the opportunity to plan and build a castle that will shelter and promote your family for generations to come.

In these challenging and changeable times, every powerful noble needs a castle! Its thick walls and high towers will display your power and influence, and provide you with a secure home where you can live comfortably and enjoy your wealth.

I will talk you through all the important things you need to consider. We master masons have been designing castles for hundreds of years, so I am an expert in castle design and I can help you plan a building that is the height of comfort and security. I'll also guide you through the main ways of defending your castle, and we'll look at some accounts of famous **sieges** to help you understand how to make your castle the strongest in the land. There is a lot to think about and time is short. So let us begin straight away!

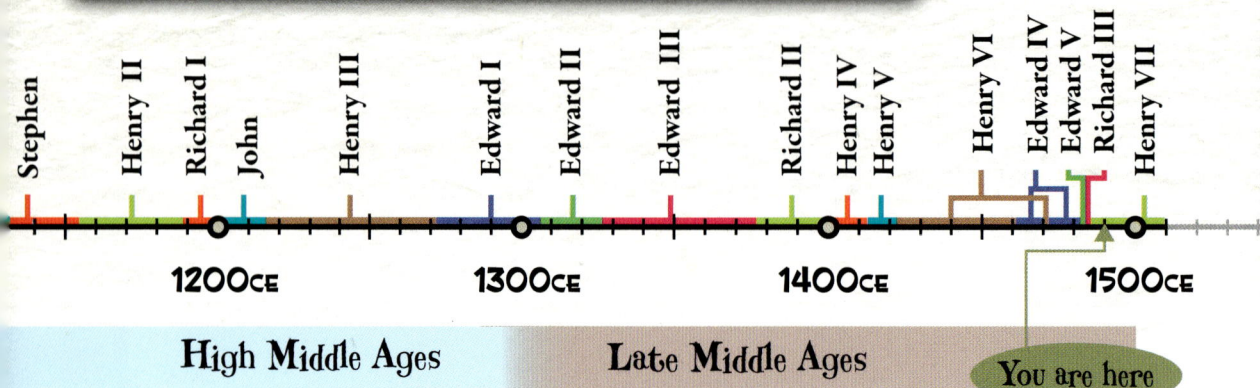

Stephen | Henry II | Richard I | John | Henry III | Edward I | Edward II | Edward III | Richard II | Henry IV | Henry V | Henry VI | Edward IV | Edward V | Richard III | Henry VII

1200ce — 1300ce — 1400ce — 1500ce

High Middle Ages | Late Middle Ages

You are here

CASTLE BUILDING BASICS

To start you off, here are a few things you'll need to consider:

Where would you like your castle to be?

What type of castle do you want?

What are the parts of your castle?

What rooms will you have in your castle?

How will you defend your castle?

Location, Location, Location

I would advise you to build your castle on top of a hill. This will allow your soldiers to see an enemy army approaching from a long way off. Being high up will also make your castle visible to people in the area, reminding them of your power.

You should also try to build your castle close to transport routes (the sea, or a river or a road), as well as sources of food and water. The site will also need to be near a quarry, where the castle workers can cut blocks of stone for the castle walls.

This is Beeston Castle in England. Castles built on top of hills are easier to defend.

Parts of a Castle

Although castles come in many different shapes and sizes, they all have the same basic parts: a central stronghold (usually a keep), walls, a gatehouse and a bailey.

Keep

At the centre of your castle will be a tower called the 'keep'. The size of the keep, and the number of floors, will depend on how much money you wish to spend. During an attack, the keep is the castle's last line of defence, so you must ensure it is strong. Also, consider placing the castle's well under the keep, so you have a source of water during a siege.

Curtain wall

Surrounding the keep will be a strong wall called the 'curtain wall', patrolled by soldiers and archers.

Bailey

The enclosed space between the wall and the keep is called the 'bailey'. This will contain outbuildings, including soldiers' barracks, workshops and horses' stables.

Outer curtain wall

For extra protection, consider building a second wall outside the first. This creates two baileys (also called 'wards'): an outer and an inner one.

CASTLE BUILDING BASICS

Gatehouse
The weakest point in the defences of any castle is its entrance, and this is where your enemy is most likely to attack. So you should build a big, strong tower around the entrance – this is called the 'gatehouse'.

Moat
To make your castle really secure, you could have a moat outside the castle walls. The moat could be filled with water or kept dry. Sometimes moats are planted with sharp stakes to keep invaders out.

Drawbridge
In front of the gatehouse will be the only bridge across the moat. This is called a 'drawbridge' because it can be drawn up in times of danger.

What Type of Castle Should You Choose?

I come from a long line of master masons who have passed on their skills from generation to generation down the centuries. Over time, my ancestors made gradual improvements to the design of their castles. You only have to look at the simple structures of early castles to see how far we've come ...

keep

bailey

motte

moat

Motte and bailey

This was the state-of-the-art castle in the 11th and 12th centuries. It had a wooden keep, surrounded by a wooden wall, built on top of a large mound of earth called a 'motte'. Next to this was a bailey, also enclosed by a wooden wall. By digging out the earth for the motte, they created a ditch which formed the castle's moat. Compared to later designs, these castles were simple and relatively cheap.

Wood or stone?

The first castles were made of wood, with walls of wood and earth. They could be built quickly, and building in wood is a lot cheaper than building in stone. The problem is that wood rots, and it also burns. As a result, most wooden castles didn't last very long. You should probably build your castle with stone!

CASTLE BUILDING BASICS

Stone castles

Stone castles, built from the 12th century onwards, can be constructed bigger, with taller towers, and they give better protection against the ravages of time, weather and enemy attack. The first stone castles had square keeps. But these proved vulnerable to **undermining**, so master masons started building round keeps.

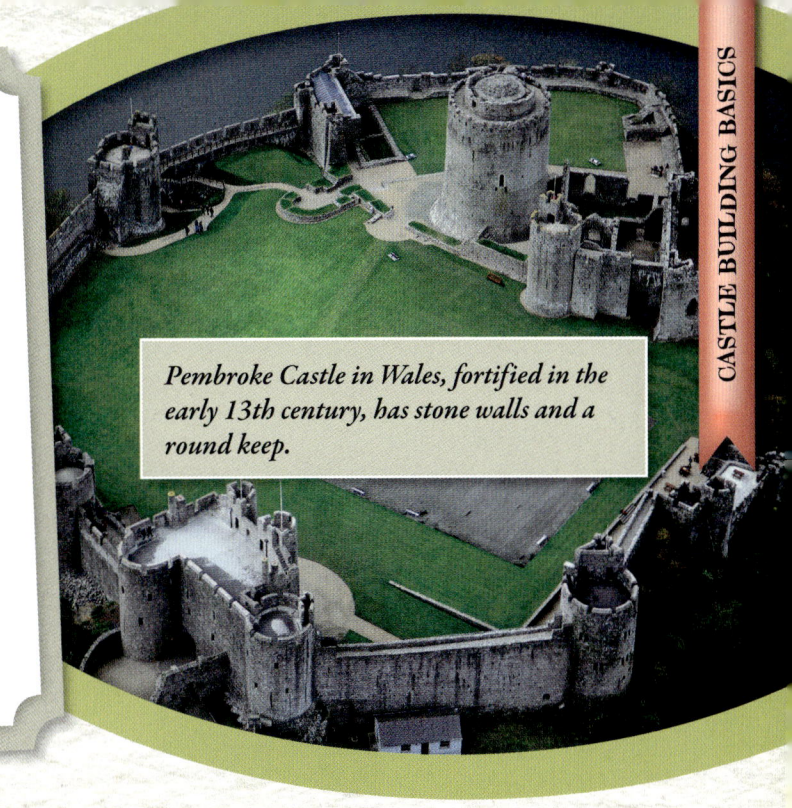

Pembroke Castle in Wales, fortified in the early 13th century, has stone walls and a round keep.

Beaumaris Castle in Wales was built in the late 13th century in a concentric style.

Concentric castles

Now we arrive at our present era of castle building. Since the 13th century, concentric castles have been all the rage. They are often called 'a castle within a castle'. They have more than one curtain wall, and each of the walls has projecting towers. Many of them don't have a central, free-standing keep. Instead, the living quarters are spread among a series of interconnected towers lining the inner wall.

9

What Rooms Will You Have in Your Castle?

Of course you will need a number of basic rooms, but you might also consider some extra ones. For example, you may wish to add a 'bower' (a lady's withdrawing room) or a 'minstrels' gallery' (a balcony above the Great Hall where musicians can play). You may even decide to have a 'bathroom' – a room set aside for bathing, would you believe! This is quite unusual though. The following are the essential rooms you will find in every castle ...

Stables
You will need horses for battle and transport, and so you will need stables. Remember to put in haylofts and sleeping quarters for grooms.

Treasury
This is where you store your coins, jewellery, fine plates and other valuable possessions.

Dungeons
Back in the early Middle Ages, castles didn't have dungeons. The whole idea of keeping prisoners would have seemed very odd. The word 'dungeon' actually comes from 'donjon', another word for the keep. So how did dungeons become prisons? Well, as time went on, castle owners started to want to live in more comfortable quarters, rather than the keep. At the same time, it became common practice to lock up troublemakers rather than kill them. As it was the most secure part of the castle, the keep became a place for storing valuables – and prisoners. The prisoners were held in the cold, dark storerooms in the basement, and these became known as the castle dungeons.

Undercroft
Another word for 'cellar'. You can use this room for storage.

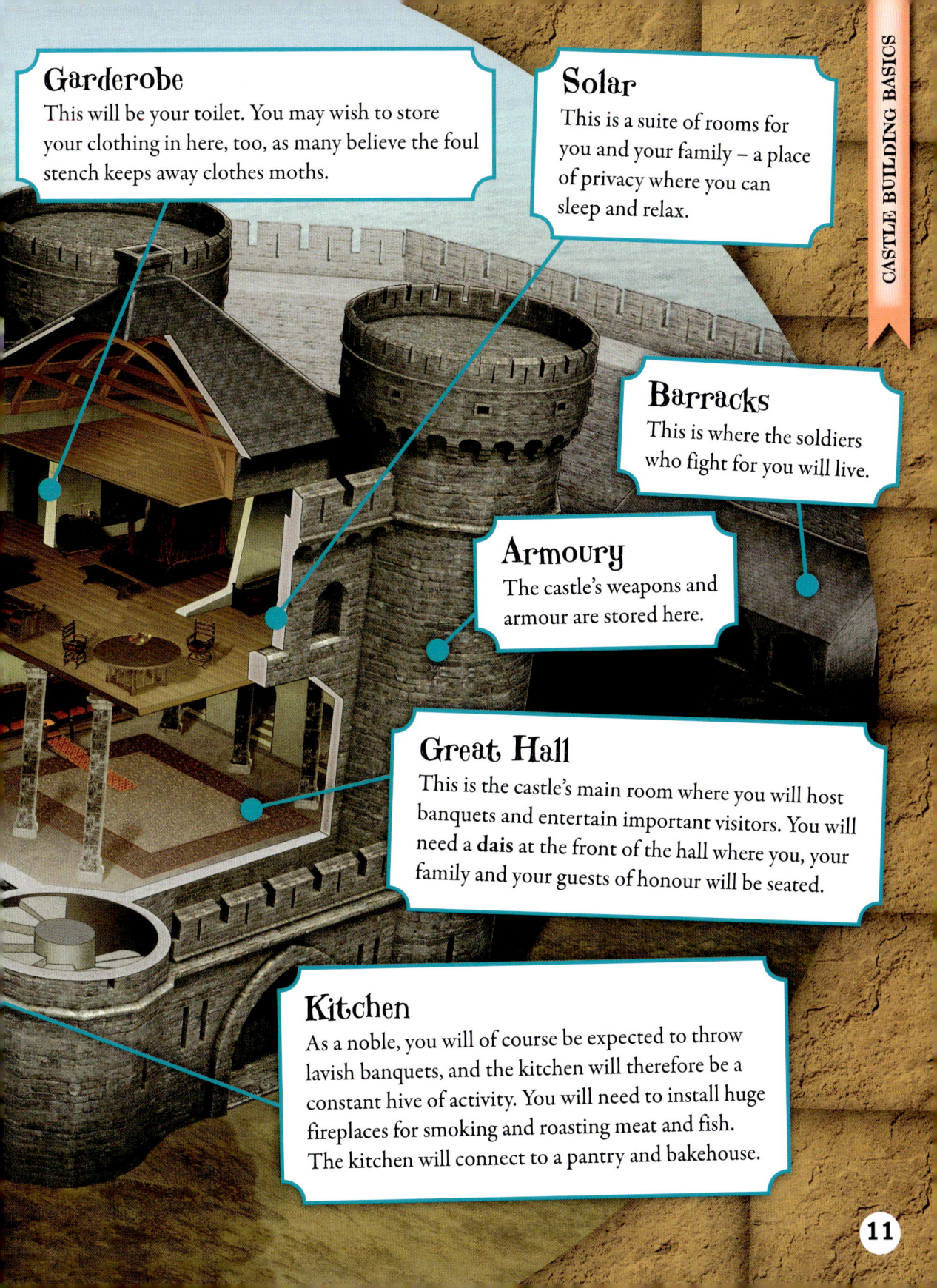

Garderobe

This will be your toilet. You may wish to store your clothing in here, too, as many believe the foul stench keeps away clothes moths.

Solar

This is a suite of rooms for you and your family – a place of privacy where you can sleep and relax.

Barracks

This is where the soldiers who fight for you will live.

Armoury

The castle's weapons and armour are stored here.

Great Hall

This is the castle's main room where you will host banquets and entertain important visitors. You will need a **dais** at the front of the hall where you, your family and your guests of honour will be seated.

Kitchen

As a noble, you will of course be expected to throw lavish banquets, and the kitchen will therefore be a constant hive of activity. You will need to install huge fireplaces for smoking and roasting meat and fish. The kitchen will connect to a pantry and bakehouse.

CASTLE BUILDING BASICS

What Will Life Be Like in Your Castle?

What kind of life can you expect to lead in your castle? One thing you can be certain of: it'll be a lot more comfortable than if you'd been living in the early Middle Ages, in the 6th–10th centuries. Castle life was pretty basic back then ...

Early Middle Ages

Castles were made of wood with no fireplaces or chimneys. Instead, the fire was in the middle of the Great Hall, which had a hole in the roof for the smoke to escape. This means the air was smoky and smelled unpleasantly of animal fat from the tallow candles. The servants could sweeten the air a little by scattering herbs on the floor and on the straw mattresses where the family slept.

Furniture was very expensive – beds were very rare! There would have been a simple long table with benches. Clothing and valuables were stored in chests. There were no separate bedrooms either – you would have slept at one end of the hall, behind a curtain.

You might not have wanted to smell the moat too closely, as the waste from the garderobe emptied directly into it.

Household

You will need lots of people to help run your castle and provide for your needs:

- castellan, or constable – will manage the day-to-day affairs of the castle and be in charge when you're away
- chamberlain – responsible for your private chamber and will supervise the servants who work there
- quartermaster – will look after supplies
- large team of servants
- carpenter
- **blacksmith**
- cook
- baker
- armourer.

Late Middle Ages

The switch from wood to stone was a big improvement, although early stone castles got very cold in winter. My ancestors fixed that problem in the late 13th century by putting in fireplaces, chimneys and glazed windows (though glass is very expensive, so windows tend to be small).

Thanks to recent increases in trade and travel, a world of luxury goods from abroad have become available to enhance a castle: **tapestries**, rugs and bedcovers to provide extra warmth and colour in those big, draughty rooms, and spices to mask bad odours. Speaking of bad odours, some things never change: the garderobes still empty into a pit or straight into the moat!

CASTLE BUILDING BASICS

Beds, bath tubs, carpets and fireplaces: castle life is definitely more comfortable in the later Middle Ages!

SPECIAL FEATURES FOR YOUR CASTLE

Learning from the Best

You'll need to think about what kind of 'look and feel' your castle will have. To give you some ideas, I've included some examples of famous castles below.

Of course, the type of castle you go for depends on your needs. Do you have a lot of enemies? If so, prioritize building strong fortifications. Or do you love inviting the royal family to visit, perhaps for a lavish banquet? That would require you to have lots of space for entertaining.

Style over substance?

You might decide that your top priority is having a castle that looks good. Bodiam Castle was built in the 1380s, and it is a fine example of a late-medieval moated castle. It doesn't have space for many soldiers, but it looks great!

Secret tunnels

Secret tunnels are a good feature to consider, either for escaping during a siege or just sneaking around. Nottingham Castle had a secret passageway which led out of the middle bailey and underneath the castle walls.

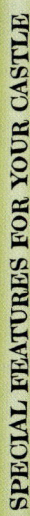

Fortified manor house

If your **budget** doesn't stretch to a full castle, you could consider a fortified manor house, like Stokesay Castle. These are basically large houses, but with some fortifications such as towers or a moat to help keep out intruders.

Coastal castle

If you trade abroad a lot, you might want to choose a coastal site like Bamburgh Castle so you can get to your ships quickly. Bear in mind, though, that castles on the coast are likely to be attacked first by any invading armies.

Upcycling

It might make sense to use an existing site. Lincoln Castle, for example, was built on the site of a pre-existing Roman fortress.

SPECIAL FEATURES FOR YOUR CASTLE

Design and Decoration

The interior design of your castle is for your own comfort and enjoyment – but also to impress your guests. As a master mason, my expertise lies in the castle design itself rather than the interiors, but having spent so much time in castles, I can help by giving you some tips on the best ways to furnish and decorate.

Decorating furniture

Some ideas to consider are:

- carving patterns
- covering it with gold leaf
- using decorative metal work
- covering it with elaborate tapestries.

Coat of arms

If your noble family has a **coat of arms**, you might want to incorporate this design into your castle furnishings – for example, painting it on to special pieces of furniture, or carving it into stone.

If you don't have a coat of arms already, why not design one? Ideally you'd get a professional in, but here's what to do if you want to make one yourself:

1. Make a list of your best features. For example, are you brave, kind, trustworthy or loyal? Make up a motto for yourself based around your best feature, for example *Kind at all times*.
2. Choose your favourite colours, e.g. gold and green.
3. Choose your favourite animal or plant, e.g. cat.
4. Combine these into a shield-shaped design.

KIND AT ALL TIMES

You can also use this as the basis of your flag design and your personal seal for sending letters.

SPECIAL FEATURES FOR YOUR CASTLE

Tapestries

Tapestries will make your castle look beautiful and will also provide **insulation** through the cold winters. Look at the Överhogdal or Bayeux tapestries for inspiration – you could tell a whole story with your tapestries, or just show a scene from your favourite book.

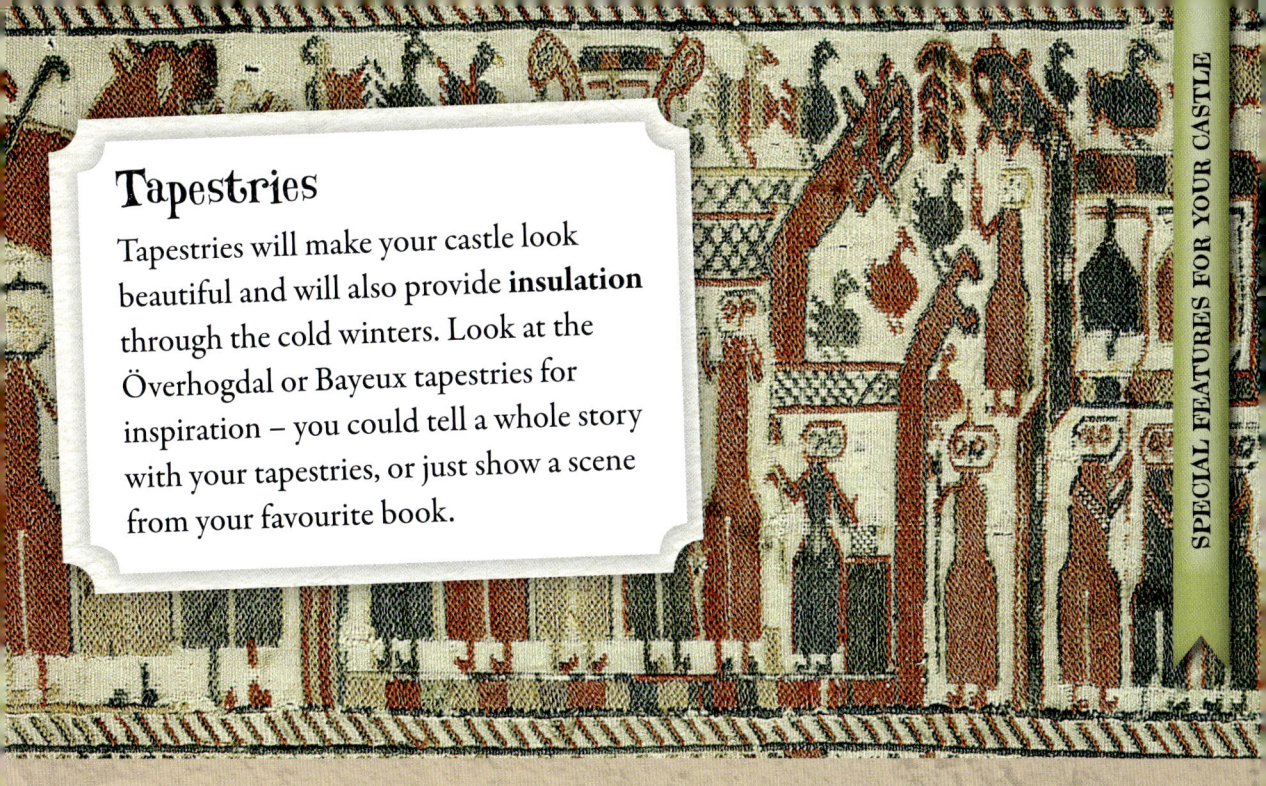

Illuminated manuscripts

How about building a collection of illuminated manuscripts? These are handwritten books with gorgeously decorated pages.

TOP TIP: If you do collect some manuscripts to display in your castle, consider chaining them to the shelves. Having been painstakingly hand-copied and decorated with the likes of **lapis lazuli** and gold, your books will be extremely valuable!

Budget

Choosing the design and decorations for your castle could get expensive. Set your budget before you start, and stick to it. If you do go over-budget, you could raise local taxes to make up the shortfall – but it won't make you very popular!

17

KEEPING OUT THE ENEMY

We've thought about the type of castle you might want, how it will look and what features it will have, but a castle is more than a grand house. You must face the possibility that one day your castle will be attacked, and prepare your defences. It goes without saying that your castle will need strong walls. I would also suggest that you consider a number of clever defensive features designed to frustrate the most determined enemy.

Moat

A water-filled ditch around your castle will slow down an advancing army, making it easier for archers on the castle walls to repel their attack. A moat also reduces the risk of the enemy tunnelling under your castle.

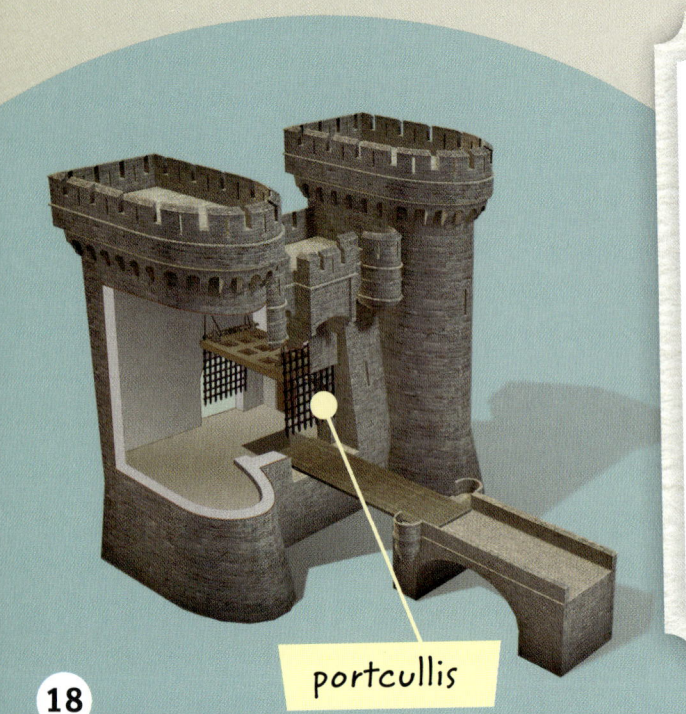

Gatehouse

Since your castle must have an entrance, you should consider how to make your gatehouse as strong as possible. Make sure it has thick wooden doors, and add an iron grille called a 'portcullis' which can be raised or lowered. Bigger castles have two portcullises, so attackers can be lured into the gatehouse and then trapped in the passage beneath it.

portcullis

Barbican

The barbican is quite a recent invention. It's another fortified structure built in front of the gatehouse containing *another* layer of portcullises that attackers must pass through to gain access to your castle.

KEEPING OUT THE ENEMY

gatehouse

barbican

Towers

Consider building towers where you can place lookouts to give you advance warning of an approaching enemy. In the early Middle Ages, these towers were square-shaped, and attackers could topple them by undermining one of the corners. These days we build round towers with none of those vulnerable corners! Round towers also make it easier to see your enemies, and their curved walls are better at deflecting missiles.

Bodiam Castle, a 14th-century English castle, has a combination of round and square towers.

Up Against the Wall

The walls of your castle will be its sturdiest defence, so you must make sure they are strong! But even the thickest stone wall can be **breached** by a determined attacker. Consider adding extra features to make your walls as strong as possible.

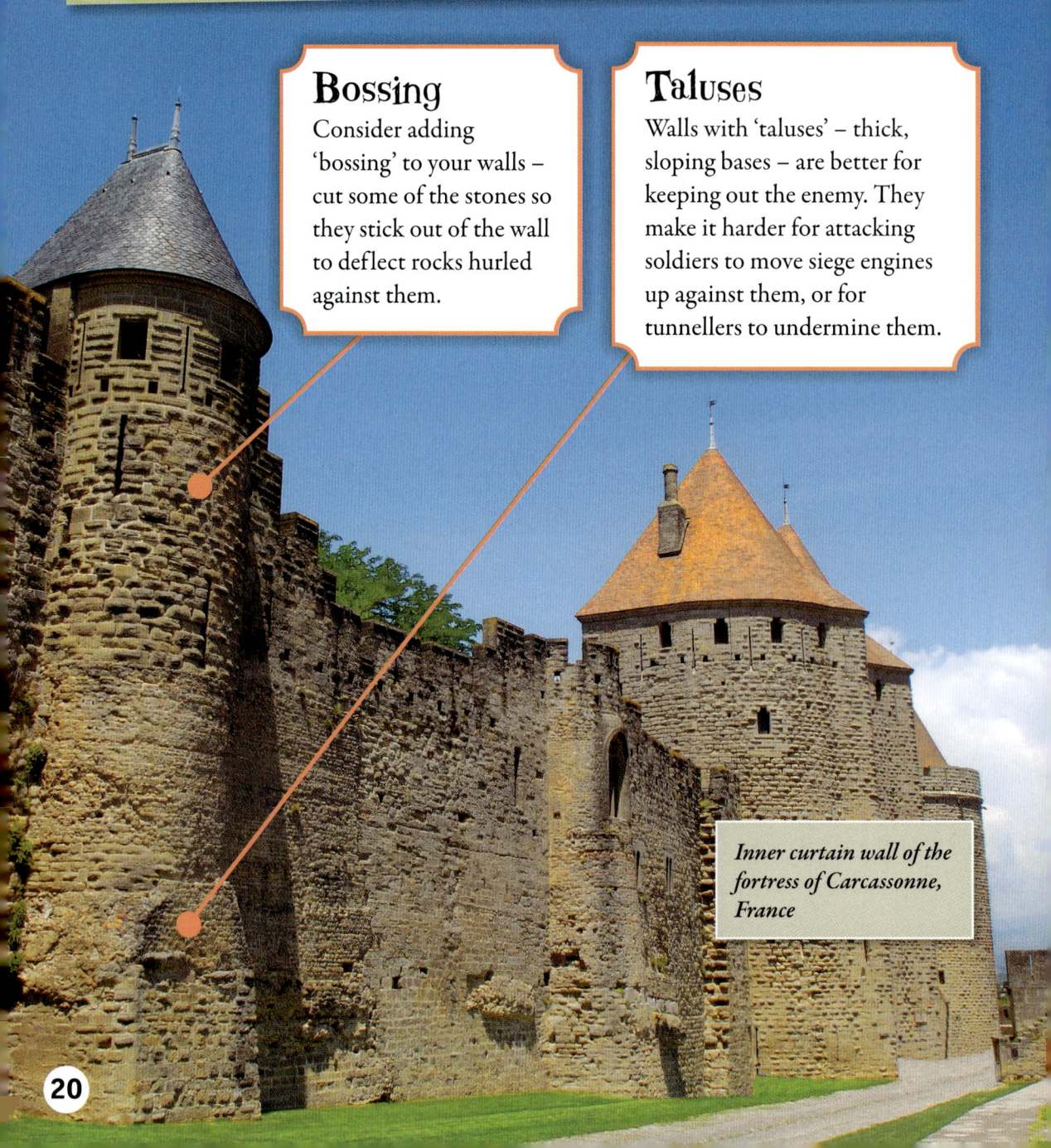

Bossing

Consider adding 'bossing' to your walls – cut some of the stones so they stick out of the wall to deflect rocks hurled against them.

Taluses

Walls with 'taluses' – thick, sloping bases – are better for keeping out the enemy. They make it harder for attacking soldiers to move siege engines up against them, or for tunnellers to undermine them.

Inner curtain wall of the fortress of Carcassonne, France

Arrow loops

These are narrow openings through which archers can fire their arrows. On the inside, the wall around the arrow loop opens widely so the archers can stand comfortably.

Arrow loop at Carreg Cennen Castle in Wales

Battlements

The tops of the castle walls should have regularly spaced openings, about 80 centimetres wide, called 'crenels'. The sections of wall between them are called 'merlons'. The crenels and merlons together form the castle's battlements and provide ideal cover for archers as they fire their arrows at an advancing enemy.

Machicolations

The battlements will jut outwards from the wall, and beneath them will be openings called 'machicolations' – through which defenders can throw or pour whatever horrible things they can find on to attackers climbing the wall.

Walkways

There should be broad paths on top of the walls along which the castle's defenders can move quickly. These walkways are usually exposed to the castle interior so that if enemy soldiers manage to climb the walls and get on to the walkways, defenders inside the castle can fire on them.

UNDER ATTACK

In the last chapter we talked about castle defences. Now we're going to look at how these defences might be tested in an enemy attack. There are two basic forms of attack: the direct assault on a castle's walls, and the bombardment of a castle from a distance by 'siege engines'. Attacking armies usually attempt both of these at the same time to achieve maximum impact. First of all, let's look at the direct assault ...

Climbing the walls

Soldiers will try to scale the walls of the castle using ladders. However, this will leave them exposed to archers. Alternatively, they may use a 'siege tower' – a tall wooden structure on wheels, which they will push up against the castle wall. This provides protection for the soldiers inside it as they climb towards the battlements. The enemy might cover their siege towers in animal hides soaked in vinegar and mud to protect them from fire.

Siege towers can be over 20 metres high.

Battering

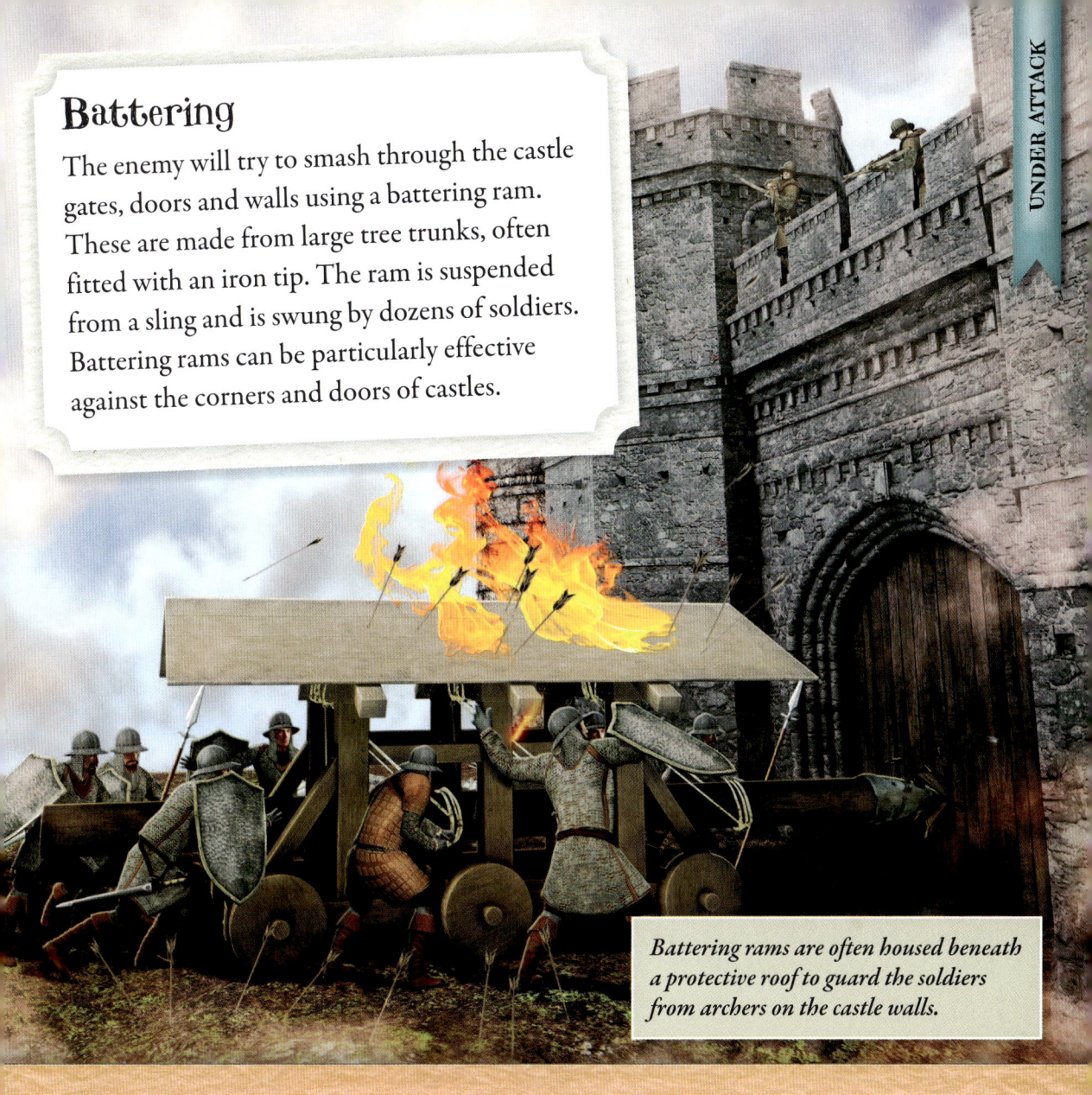

The enemy will try to smash through the castle gates, doors and walls using a battering ram. These are made from large tree trunks, often fitted with an iron tip. The ram is suspended from a sling and is swung by dozens of soldiers. Battering rams can be particularly effective against the corners and doors of castles.

Battering rams are often housed beneath a protective roof to guard the soldiers from archers on the castle walls.

Tunnelling

If attackers can't go over or through the castle's walls, they may try tunnelling beneath them. They might emerge into the bailey in a surprise attack, or undermine the wall above by filling the tunnel with logs smeared with animal fat and setting light to them. This destroys the foundations of the wall, causing it to collapse.

While they are being dug, the tunnels are supported by wooden props. If their plan is to undermine the walls, the attackers will set fire to the props as well.

Bombarding Your Castle

As well as trying to break through the castle's walls, an enemy might also bombard the castle with missiles launched from enormous siege engines. Here are three different types of siege engine you need to watch out for.

Trebuchets

The trebuchet is the most powerful of all siege engines and can hurl stones weighing 90 kilograms up to 275 metres.

Mangonel

The mangonel, like the trebuchet, is a kind of giant catapult. It is lighter and more manoeuvrable than the trebuchet.

Ballista

The ballista is like a giant crossbow. It is less powerful but much more accurate – and it's quicker to reset after it's been fired.

A Fair Fight?

If you believe there is anything honourable about a castle siege, then think again. Sieges are supposed to be governed by the rules of **chivalry**, and they usually are ... at the start. Before hostilities begin, attackers should offer the castle a chance to surrender. If this is accepted, then the castle inhabitants should be allowed to leave the castle unharmed. If the castle doesn't surrender within a specified time, however, the siege begins. After that, the **besiegers** will do anything to capture the castle – and defenders will do everything they can to hold on to it.

Treachery

Castles can be betrayed by traitors within them. It happened during the siege of Antioch in 1098. Despite months of bombardment, the attackers could not break into the city. Finally, they bribed a guard, who let them climb the city walls at night.

It happened again in 1480, during the siege of Rhodes, when someone inside the island fortress signalled to their friends in the besieging army and the city was nearly captured.

LEARNING FROM THE PAST

Let's look at some real-life sieges from the 13th century. How well did the castle defences work? What tactics did both sides use? This could help us when it comes to designing your castle.

Setting the scene

After the Battle of Hastings in 1066 and the Norman Conquest, King William I had conquered the Saxons and ruled over England and **Normandy** – as did the next five kings who came after him. There followed many battles between England and France; the English kings tried to take over large areas of France and the French kings tried to reclaim their lands.

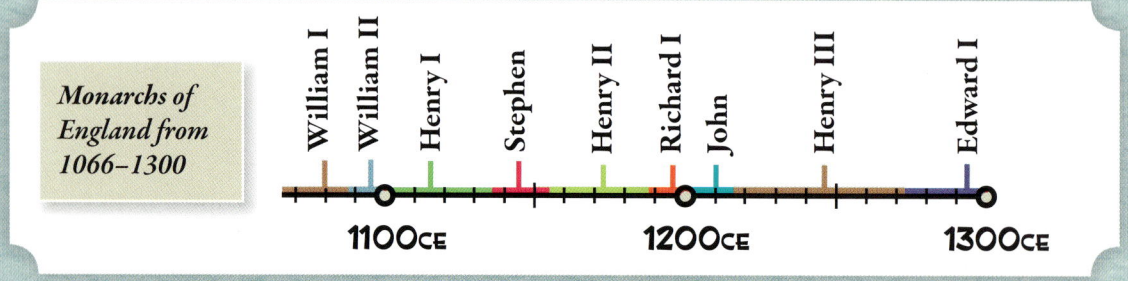

Monarchs of England from 1066–1300

William I | William II | Henry I | Stephen | Henry II | Richard I | John | Henry III | Edward I

1100CE — 1200CE — 1300CE

Kings relied on noblemen to fight battles and defend lands on their behalf. William the Conqueror had made lots of his Norman followers into nobles called 'barons', and they built strong castles in order to show off their power and keep control of the people. But because the barons were so powerful, it was important to keep them happy – which not every king managed to do ...

So, in the 13th century the English kings were fighting battles against France and sometimes fighting against their own barons too. Let's look at some of the sieges which took place in the 1200s to learn more and to see how having good castle defences can change the course of history!

The Siege of Castle Gaillard, 1203–4

Our first famous siege began in 1203, when King John was on the throne of England. He also ruled Normandy, where Castle Gaillard is located. The castle was held by the baron Roger de Lacy, who was loyal to King John.

King Philip II of France wanted to conquer Normandy and take it back from King John, but to do so he needed to capture Castle Gaillard. Could he get through the castle's many layers of defences?

King John fact file

- Youngest son of King Henry II
- Became King after his brother Richard I ('Richard the Lionheart')
- Ruled from 1199–1216
- Agreed to sign Magna Carta (see p32)

LEARNING FROM THE PAST

Castle Gaillard has formidable defences: built on a high hill above the River Seine, its keep is protected by a triangular barbican and two curtain walls.

First, the English defenders of the castle tried to prevent King Philip's forces from crossing the river.

"Your Majesty, the English have destroyed the bridge."

Philip uses boats to form a bridge.

"Be off, English! You will not destroy our bridge of boats!"

Soon the French forces have crossed the river and surrounded the castle. The English commander of the castle, Roger de Lacy, and his wife Maud are worried …

"The French are settling in for a long siege. I hope we have enough supplies to last us."

"Everyone who isn't needed for the fight should leave the castle. Then we will have fewer mouths to feed."

"I hope they'll be all right."

"King Philip has given his word not to harm them."

Once those not needed for the battle have left, the siege begins.

LEARNING FROM THE PAST

While the siege is being fought above ground, French soldiers are quietly beginning a tunnel …

I hope they don't hear us.

The French manage to break through the barbican wall by tunnelling underneath it.

Quick! Let's open the gate so we can let our soldiers through!

The French have made it into the outer bailey, but still have another two walls to get through.

The ladders are too short! We are done for!

29

30

"I could climb through there and let everyone in through the gates."

"You realize that leads to the toilet!"

"How did you get inside?"

"You don't want to know, Your Majesty!"

And now King Philip's army face the third and final wall of the castle.

"How are we going to get through that?"

"Tunnel under the wall, using that bridge as cover!"

"Yes, Your Majesty."

After the final wall is breached, the castle quickly falls. On 6th March 1204, after an eight-month siege, Roger de Lacy and his fellow defenders surrender to King Philip.

So what lesson can we learn from the fall of Castle Gaillard? Keep an eye out for miners digging secret tunnels, and watch out for unguarded entry points! Of course every castle needs garderobes, but we should make sure that they can all be seen from the turrets or are obstructed by iron bars.

The Siege of Rochester Castle, 1215

After he lost Normandy to King Philip of France, things just got worse for King John. Back in England, the barons rebelled against him and John had to go to war with them to defend his place on the throne. This newspaper-style account of the siege of Rochester Castle will tell you more, as well as showing how crucial it is for your castle to have a really strong keep.

LEARNING FROM THE PAST

THE TOWN CRIER

Wednesday 14th October 1215

KING JOHN LAYS SIEGE TO ROCHESTER

Rebel barons holed up at Rochester were fighting for their lives last night as King John's forces began assaulting the mighty walls of the castle with a deadly barrage of rocks and stones.

***

A RIGHT ROYAL ROW

The spat between the King and his barons kicked off back in 1204 when John lost most of his lands in Normandy and France. To get them back he needed money, so he hit the barons with a huge tax bill. The angry barons struck back by forcing the King to agree to a list of demands called 'Magna Carta'.

When John tried to back out of the agreement, the barons threatened to hand the English throne to Prince Louis of France. For John, that was the final straw. He decided to march on the barons' stronghold in London. In his way lay Rochester Castle …

* * *

BRIDGE DESTROYED

When the King's men entered the city last Sunday night, their first act was to wreck the bridge over the River Medway to foil any relief efforts aimed at saving the rebel barons. They then **sacked** Rochester Cathedral, before laying siege to the castle.

* * *

STATE OF THE REBELS

There's no word as yet from rebel chief William d'Aubigny, Lord of Belvoir. But our chronicler on the scene, Roger of Wendover, estimates there are between 95 and 140 knights currently inside the castle, along with crossbowmen, sergeants, foot soldiers and others.

* * *

According to eyewitnesses, the King has no less than five siege engines trained on the fortress, supported by archers and crossbowmen, and they're giving it everything they've got. 'We will break down those walls, make no mistake!' vowed Captain Savari de Mauléon of the royal army.

▲
One of the copies of Magna Carta signed in 1215

WHAT IS MAGNA CARTA?

Magna Carta is a list of rules and promises. It says that everybody has to obey the law, including the **monarch**. It also says that all 'free men' have the right to justice and a fair trial. A source close to King John has suggested he didn't think Magna Carta was very important when he signed it, but it is already proving to be of great national importance.

5th November 1215

ROYAL ARMY BREACHES CASTLE WALL!

Forces loyal to King John were cheering last night as the wall of Rochester Castle finally fell and they captured the bailey. It was the climax of a ferocious three-week campaign involving siege engines, crossbow fire and risky tunnelling.

TUNNEL TRIUMPH

'We order you to make, by day and night, all the pickaxes you can and send them to us at Rochester with all speed.'

That was the King's order, sent out to all the blacksmiths of Canterbury on 14th October. Within days the tunnelling tools began to arrive and the miners got to work, digging patiently beneath the castle walls while the trebuchets and mangonels kept the defenders distracted. Yesterday the tunnel was complete and the soldiers poured through, quickly overwhelming the defenders.

RETREAT TO THE KEEP

The besieged barons have now taken refuge in the keep. **Royalist** officer William Marshal, 1st Earl of Pembroke, is optimistic that the battle is nearly won. 'We'll flush them out of there by the weekend,' he predicts.

The keep is square, measuring 21 by 21 metres, with turrets at each corner.

LEARNING FROM THE PAST

26th November 1215

King demolishes part of keep with help from ... animal fat!

King John moved a step closer to victory over the renegade barons yesterday when he brought down an entire corner of Rochester Castle's keep.

THWARTED

For weeks the royal troops have been thwarted by the keep's immensely thick walls. Finally, John came up with a plan.

Facing increasing pressure to defeat the rebels, who were still defiantly holding out against all odds, the King tried a new tactic: he used animal grease to start a fire under the building.

COLLAPSE

The King's miners dug beneath the keep's south-east turret, then filled the tunnel with **tinder** smeared with the animal fat before setting it alight. Soon, a whole corner of the building fell and as the dust cleared, the royal troops rushed into the gaping hole.

But the rebels retreated behind a thick wall into the northern half of the interior, where they are continuing their stubborn resistance.

UNUSUAL DESIGN

The rebels were saved by the unusual design of the keep, which has a thick wall built through its centre, splitting the building in two.

▲ *Artist's impression of the keep's collapse*

THE TROUBADOUR

Tuesday, 1st December 1215

SPECIAL SOUVENIR EDITION

ROCHESTER REBELS SURRENDER

After nearly two months trapped inside Rochester Castle, the rebel **garrison** laid down their arms yesterday and surrendered to the forces of King John. In the end it wasn't siege engines or battering rams that defeated them, but hunger …

Emerging from the keep with their arms raised, the survivors appeared pale and weak from lack of food, yet they managed to keep their pride and dignity, winning the respect of their former foes. One elderly chronicler, who has witnessed more than his share of castle sieges, was heard to say: 'Our age has not known a siege so hard-pressed nor so bravely resisted … '

According to unconfirmed reports, the King initially planned to execute all the rebels, but was dissuaded from doing so by his chief advisor, Captain Savari de Mauléon.

Perhaps the captain feared that this would lead to revenge killings of the royalist prisoners in rebel prisons.

We understand the remaining rebels are currently under guard, awaiting transportation to the dungeons of Corfe Castle and other castles controlled by the King.

So, the defence of Rochester was undermined by … undermining! Our main takeaway from this siege is the importance of building on rock, or surrounding your castle with a moat – anything to thwart those terrifying tunnellers!

LEARNING FROM THE PAST

The Siege of Dover Castle, 1216–17

The year after King John's troops had captured Rochester Castle from them, the rebel barons offered to help the French prince, Louis, become King of England instead. However, many English nobles remained loyal to King John, including Hubert de Burgh, Earl of Kent, the commander of Dover Castle.

Dover Castle is one of my all-time favourites. The biggest castle in England, its defences are truly spectacular: a square keep with two curtain walls and a gatehouse on the northern side, plus a wooden barbican surrounded by a ditch and a **stockade** of thick oak posts. In 1216–17, the defences were tested as never before in two sieges by Prince Louis of France.

I have uncovered the diaries of two soldiers: one of them in Louis's besieging army, and the other fighting for Hubert de Burgh to defend Dover Castle. Let's see how the castle's defences held up.

20th June 1216

We landed in Kent in May, and it has been success after success for the French army. The cowardly 'King' John fled as soon as we arrived, and we marched towards London where the English barons proclaimed Louis as King.

The royal castles of Canterbury, Rochester and Winchester have all given in to us — however, one castle still resists: Dover Castle is still loyal to the false King John. We are marching there now — I can hardly wait. It will be another shining victory for our army, and then Louis will truly be King of all England.

8th July 1216

These are worrying times for me and my fellow soldiers in the garrison at Dover Castle. Ever since the **pretender** Louis landed on English soil, we've been gathering supplies and preparing for a siege, knowing that the French will have to take this fortress before their victory is complete.

LEARNING FROM THE PAST

22nd July 1216

Just a few days ago, we stood on the battlements and watched as Louis's army marched into view, his blue and gold banners streaming in the sea breeze. We were filled with trepidation – but then they did nothing except parade back and forth in front of the castle! Eventually our commander, Hubert de Burgh, got fed up and ordered some of us to dash out of the castle, capture one of the French crossbowmen and throw him into the dungeons. This made Louis furious, and he began the siege in earnest!

As I write, the walls are trembling as the French trebuchets and mangonels send huge stones against us. I hope that if our stockade walls stand firm, we may yet hold out against them ...

2nd August 1216

The siege is going very well!

Louis commanded the army to set up camp outside the castle and send everything we had against them: siege engines and tall towers full of crossbowmen — and all the while, a small group of us were secretly tunnelling underneath the stockade. Once the tunnel was finished, I set fire to the wooden supports and we sprinted back out so we could watch the wall come tumbling down. As soon as the wall fell, we charged through the gap. The barbican was ours!

We have now begun digging beneath the eastern tower of the North Gate. I like to imagine Hubert de Burgh and the English soldiers standing in the bailey, watching cracks appear in the tower, unable to stop us digging away at its foundations from below.

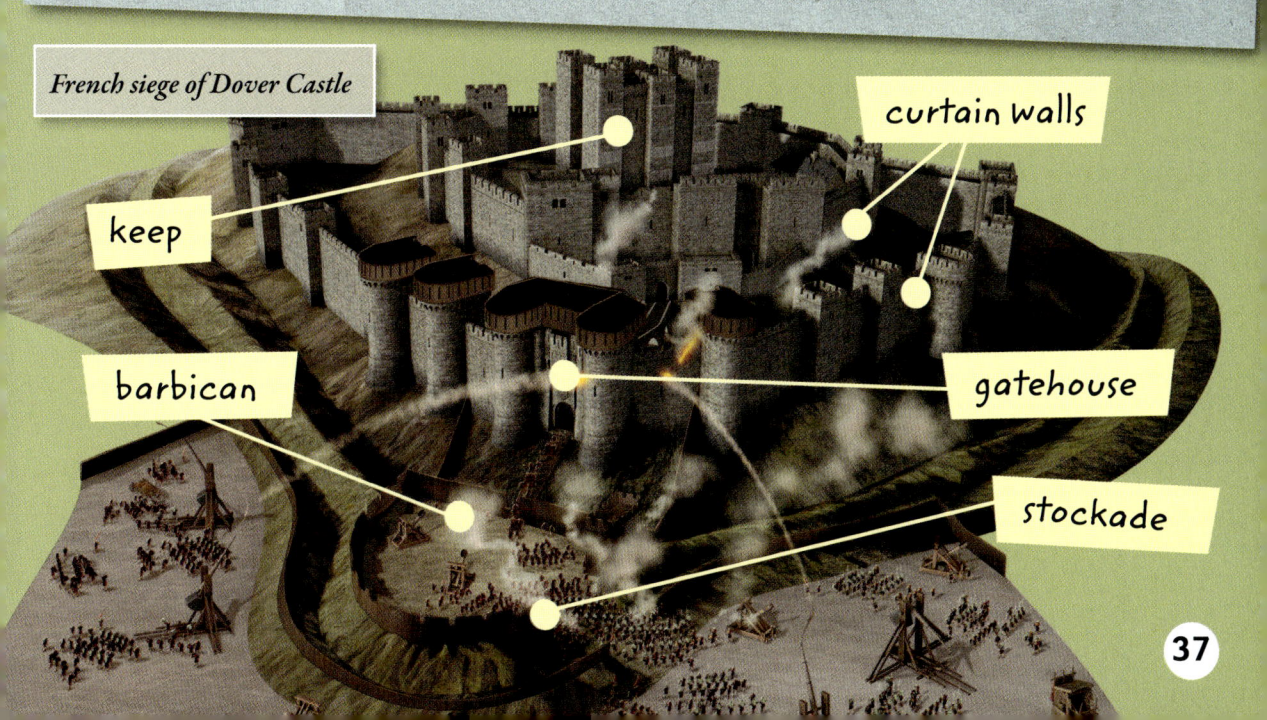

French siege of Dover Castle

- keep
- curtain walls
- barbican
- gatehouse
- stockade

37

28th August 1216

The siege is not going well!

Today the eastern tower collapsed, great stone blocks crashing to the floor, and our army surged through the gap, ready to take the castle. We had done it!

... Or so we thought, until we met a strong line of defenders who began to drive us out of the castle. We had to fall back, and they quickly repaired the wall behind us, stripping timbers from other parts of the castle to block the gap.

I caught sight of King Louis as we trudged back to our tents. He was simmering with rage at our defeat. We are determined to break this castle though, no matter how long it takes! I think we are in for a long, drawn-out siege as we wait for them to get hungry enough to surrender.

10th October 1216

It has been nearly three months since the siege began, and we have fought well and bravely. But now we are fighting an invisible enemy within the walls – within our very bellies. Three months is a long time to eat only pickled beef and biscuits. It is a long time to be hungry.

14th October 1216

Today Hubert de Burgh signed a truce with Louis, and our ordeal is finally over. It's not clear what is going to happen next, but it's such a relief to have enough fresh food to eat – I don't think we could have lasted much longer.

25th October 1216

Today we received word that King John has died. We all wondered if Hubert de Burgh would surrender Dover Castle to Louis, but he has stayed loyal to John's son, Prince Henry. Henry may only be nine, but he is the rightful King of England. We even heard that Louis offered Hubert all of East Anglia if he surrendered, but he was not swayed. Louis has abandoned the siege, and has left for London.

I have heard whisperings that Hubert doesn't intend to keep his truce and plans to make things very difficult for the French army. That doesn't seem very honourable to me, but I suppose I'm no great lord and I don't know how these things work.

LEARNING FROM THE PAST

1st May 1217

We gave up trying to break Dover Castle, moving on to other targets. But Hubert and his garrison continued to be a thorn in our side — the castle's position on the south-east coast means they control the English Channel. Whenever ships try to sail across from France with reinforcements or supplies, Hubert's soldiers fight them off and raid the supplies.

Our great King Louis has had to admit that we cannot conquer England without Dover Castle, and so we are marching back — this time armed with a new secret weapon. It is called 'malvoisin,' which the English translate as 'evil neighbour,' and it's a bit like a trebuchet. Louis says that not even Dover Castle can withstand its power! Now we will defeat them once and for all!

12th May 1217

Louis and the French army have come back, this time with a new, huge catapult ... but it makes no difference! The walls of Dover Castle still hold firm, and we have burned their siege towers and seized their supplies.

23rd May 1217

Today we got news that the French army has been defeated at Lincoln. Things were already looking bad for Louis, and this turned out to be the final straw. He and his army have turned tail and scuttled back to France!

Dover Castle has helped to stop the French invasion – I can see why they call this castle 'the key to England'. Now I hope that life can return to normal.

The most dangerous moment in this siege was the undermining of the eastern tower. Helped by strong leadership from Hubert de Burgh, the defenders stood firm. Once they had driven out the attackers, they plugged the gap with timbers taken from other parts of the castle.

The Siege of Kenilworth Castle, 1266

You must consider that however strong you make your castle, there is one more strategy an enemy could use: they could play the waiting game. By surrounding a castle with their forces for weeks or even months on end, they can try to starve the castle inhabitants into surrender ...

King John's son Henry, who was a boy during the siege of Dover Castle, grew up to become King Henry III. Just like his father, he had a war with his barons over how he was running the country.

In 1266, in the midst of this war, Henry laid siege to the rebel stronghold at Kenilworth Castle, a mighty fortress in the heart of England. I have discovered a bundle of letters which were sent during the siege – some of them have been torn or have rotted away, but they still give us quite a revealing picture of the siege. Let's see if they offer any useful hints about how best to defend a castle.

outer bailey wall

keep

Kenilworth Castle has been added to over the centuries, but some features from the 13th century survive today.

From Henry, King of England, to Henry de Hastings

King Henry III

Baron Henry de Hastings

21st June 1266

Although you are the leader of the rebels and have been fighting against me, I wish to offer you peace. I swear that if you and your fellow barons will accept my authority as your **sovereign**, throw down your arms and yield this castle, I will not attack you and I will let you go your way in peace. Those of you who have lost your lands during this war will have the opportunity to buy them back.

I warn you, this is my final offer. If you refuse me, I will lay siege to this castle and defeat you.

Be in no doubt of my determination to win. I have four siege camps surrounding you. I have nine siege machines – trebuchets, mangonels and ballistas. I have three siege towers, 2000 wooden screens to protect my soldiers as they charge your walls, and 60 000 crossbow bolts. What is more, I can replenish my resources at any time if need be. You, of course, cannot.

I therefore urge you to use your common sense. Throw open your gates and end this rebellion, which has been the cause of so much misery and bloodshed.

Your friend and sovereign,

Henry

From Henry de Hastings, to King Henry

23rd June 1266

My lord, I thank you for your offer, but my answer, as before, is no. I hold this castle in the name of your sister Eleanor, Countess of Leicester, widow of our **slain** leader Simon de Montfort. I recognize no authority but hers, and if I am to surrender the castle it will be to her, not you.

We have sufficient food to hold out for many months. We have a garrison of more than 1000 battle-hardened soldiers eager for the fight, and we have siege engines of our own.

What is more, we occupy a castle with strong defences: thick stone walls and a large lake to the south and west, protecting it from your soldiers. The water protection continues with ditches along the north side and a pond to the east, so there is no place for your miners to tunnel. In short, we are secure and confident that we can withstand the very worst you can throw at us.

I have consulted with my garrison, Your Majesty, and we speak as one when we say: *We will stand firm!*

Henry de Hastings

From Henry, King of England, to Henry de Hastings

25th June 1266

You have left me with no choice. I have given orders this day for the siege to begin. As I write this, I can hear outside my tent the creak and snap of our trebuchets as they hurl huge stones to crack your walls. I hear the whisper of a hundred crossbow bolts soaring towards the soldiers on your battlements. We are bombarding you from all four of our camps in a continuous hail of missiles. This shall not cease until we see the white flag of surrender flying from your keep.

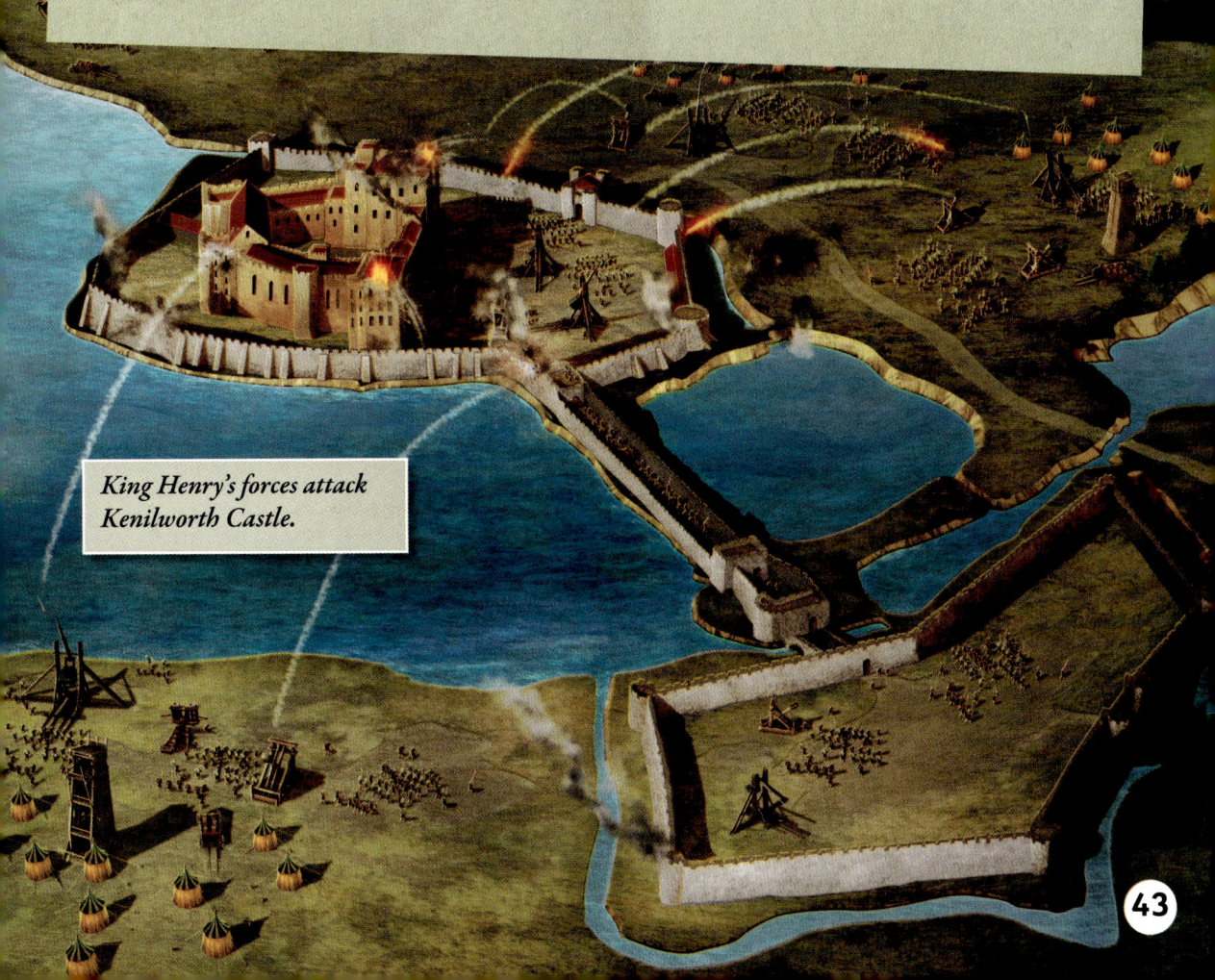

King Henry's forces attack Kenilworth Castle.

LEARNING FROM THE PAST

From Henry de Hastings,
to King Henry

30th June 1266

Do your worst, my lord. We can take it! We are secure here behind our lake. Your siege engines lack the range to reach across our watery defences and hurt us. As for your siege towers bristling with crossbowmen, they have become the targets of our own war engines.

From Henry, King of England, to the Worshipful Company of Carpenters, London

Coat of arms of the Worshipful Company of Carpenters

7th July 1266

Sirs, I hereby demand that you send me with all speed:

- one new siege tower, taller than the ones you previously built for me, with separate compartments for archers
- two new trebuchets, bigger and with greater range than those previously supplied

LEARNING FROM THE PAST

From Henry, King of England, to Prince Edward, Duke of Gascony

Prince Edward, Duke of Gascony

15th July 1266

My beloved son, as you must know, we are not finding it easy to besiege Kenilworth Castle. Kenilworth is well defended, not least because of improvements to its defences made by my father more than half a century ago. The rebels are striking back hard with their own weapons, and this siege is becoming costly in both blood and gold. The lake has been the rebels' salvation thus far. Perhaps we can overcome it. A night attack across the water might surprise them. For that we will need boats, which are not a common sight here in Warwickshire, far from the sea! Can we build some, or bring some in from the coast?

In July, an order went out from the King for barges to be brought overland from Chester, nearly 130 kilometres away. They arrived a fortnight later. So how did this lake assault work out?

From Henry de Hastings, to King Henry

4th August 1266

I applaud your efforts, my lord. The night-time barge attack across the lake was bold and imaginative. You almost took us by surprise. Yet you failed to breach our walls. Our soldiers fought back fiercely, and we were able to repel you. Once again we have proved the supremacy of our defences.

*From Henry, King of England,
to Henry de Hastings*

31st October 1266

It is now more than four months since we embarked upon this siege. The weather has turned grim. The mood in my camps, I will confess, is not much brighter. I dare not imagine what conditions must be like within your castle.

It is time we brought an end to this wretched siege.

If you lay down your arms and surrender:

- We will allow your garrison to leave the castle unmolested.
- We will offer your men the opportunity to buy back their lands once they have paid a fine.
- The amount of the fine shall be set according to each individual's involvement in the rebellion: the greater the involvement, the steeper the fine.
- These terms apply to everyone in the castle except yourself, sir. You are to be imprisoned at my pleasure for an indefinite period of time.
- You will sign a peace treaty, fixing these terms and restoring royal power to me.

From Henry de Hastings, to King Henry

1st November 1266

We cannot accept your terms as they are intolerable. To my own fate I am reconciled, but the fine you demand from many of my comrades – five times the annual yield of their lands – is far too high.

From Henry, King of England, to Henry de Hastings

2nd November 1266

Your rejection of our generous offer saddens me. There will be no revision to the terms of the treaty. Chivalry demands we grant you a further forty days' grace. You have until 11th December to surrender. If not, we shall storm the castle, and you and your fellow rebels can expect no mercy.

Things were now looking desperate for Henry de Hastings and those inside Kenilworth Castle. Henry de Hastings wrote to Eleanor, the widow of the rebel baron Simon de Montfort, with the bad news ...

LEARNING FROM THE PAST

From Henry de Hastings
to Eleanor, Countess of Leicester,
Montargis Abbey, France

Eleanor, Countess of Leicester

12th December 1266

My noble Countess – I, Henry, First Baron Hastings, send you greetings and eternal blessings.

I have endeavoured to stay true to the spirit of your late husband, Simon de Montfort, and continue to nurture the flame of his rebellion against the despot Henry III. Together with my fellow barons, I have held out at Kenilworth Castle against the King's forces for nearly six months.

Our defence of this fortress has been stubborn. Henry has failed to break down our walls, much less our spirit. Alas, now our food has nearly run out, and many of us have died from starvation or illness.

It grieves me to say this, but for the sake of those who remain, I feel duty-bound to surrender. The terms the King has offered are harsh in the extreme, yet we have no choice but to accept them.

I write this, my lady, so that you may know the truth of our story, and know that we continued your husband's fight to the bitter end. I hope we have honoured his memory with our sacrifice here at Kenilworth.

Now I must bid you farewell.

Your most loyal servant,
Henry de Hastings

From Henry, King of England, to Henry de Hastings

13th December 1266

I accept your surrender. Your soldiers fought with honour and deserve our respect as they depart the castle. I therefore guarantee your men's safety when they leave. They may take their weapons and horses. My men are under oath not to jeer at or harass them, but to maintain a respectful silence as they go their way. As for you, sir, I have given orders that you shall be escorted to my camp where we will meet to discuss your future.

LEARNING FROM THE PAST

King Henry III died six years later in 1272. Henry de Hastings died in captivity in 1269.

Although the defenders lost, in another sense they won – or at least the castle did – because the attackers never managed to break through their defences in nearly six months of trying. I would put this down to Kenilworth's excellent water protection. Also, it doesn't hurt for defenders to have a few siege engines of their own.

49

BUILDING YOUR CASTLE

So now we've completed our historical tour of famous castle sieges, it's time to design your own castle!

Paperwork

Before you can start, it helps to have a 'licence to crenellate'. This is a document signed and sealed by your monarch, giving permission for your castle to be built. You don't actually need this licence to build a castle, but having it is a way of demonstrating your high status. It also shows you are on friendly terms with your monarch.

Decisions, decisions

Think about the victories and defeats of the sieges of Castle Gaillard, Rochester Castle, Dover Castle and Kenilworth Castle. Do they help you to decide what sort of castle defences you'd like?

All my castles will offer the basics, such as strong walls and a secure keep. But there are other factors that only you will know about. For example, what sort of terrain will you be building on, and what sort of enemy are you expecting? Here's a flow chart that might help you reach your decision.

BUILDING YOUR CASTLE

HOW ARE YOU EXPECTING YOUR ENEMY TO ATTACK?

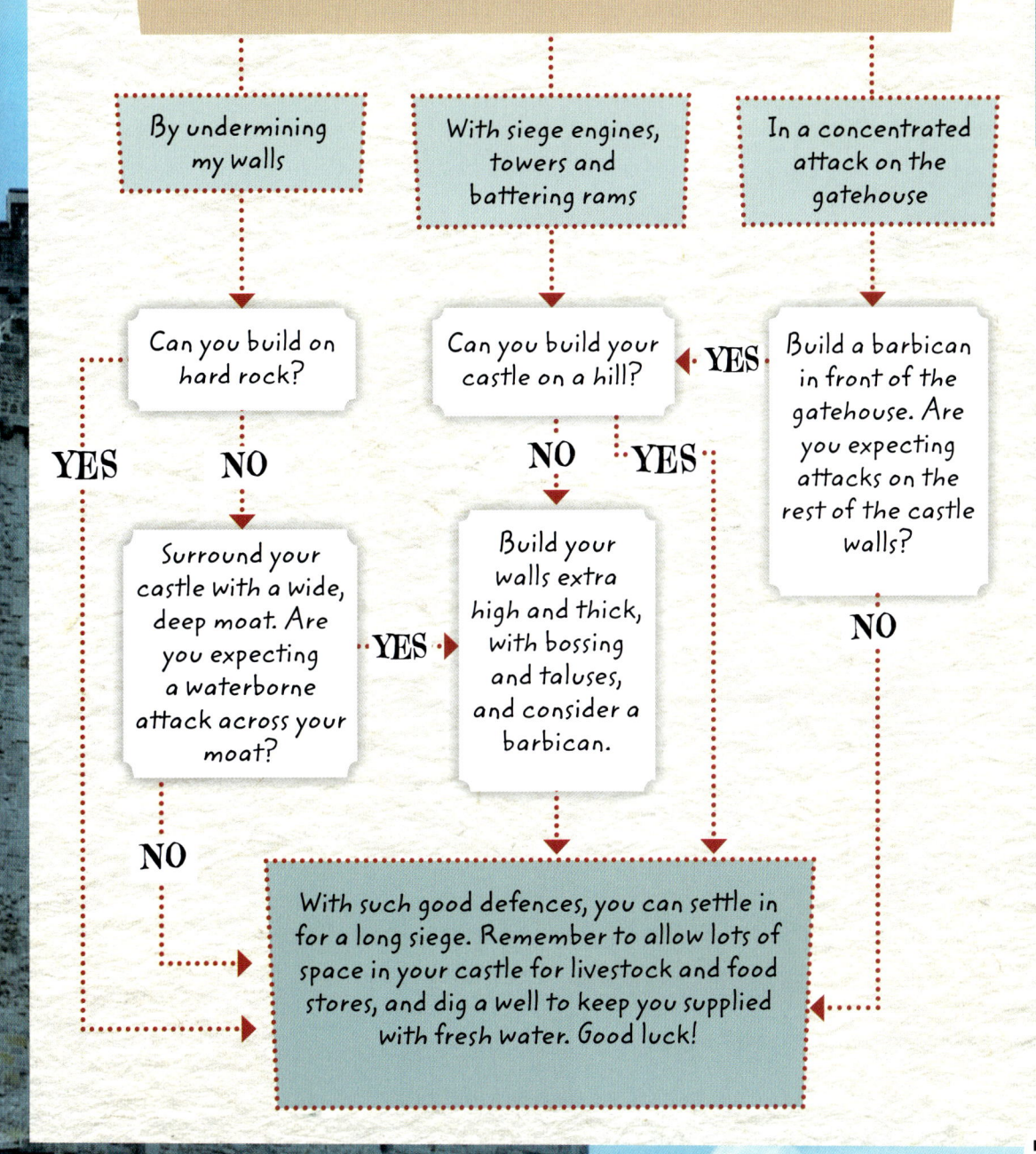

- By undermining my walls
- With siege engines, towers and battering rams
- In a concentrated attack on the gatehouse

By undermining my walls → Can you build on hard rock?
- YES →
- NO → Surround your castle with a wide, deep moat. Are you expecting a waterborne attack across your moat?
  - YES →
  - NO →

With siege engines, towers and battering rams → Can you build your castle on a hill?
- NO →
- YES → Build your walls extra high and thick, with bossing and taluses, and consider a barbican.

In a concentrated attack on the gatehouse → Build a barbican in front of the gatehouse. Are you expecting attacks on the rest of the castle walls?
- YES ← (back to "Can you build your castle on a hill?")
- NO →

With such good defences, you can settle in for a long siege. Remember to allow lots of space in your castle for livestock and food stores, and dig a well to keep you supplied with fresh water. Good luck!

51

Cost

Of course I cannot tell you how much your castle will cost until we have agreed on the kind of castle you want, but I can give you a general idea of what you can expect to pay.

Your cheapest option would be to build something very basic – little more than a keep surrounded by a wall. A much bigger castle, like Dover Castle, would cost around 35 times as much. The very biggest, such as Castle Gaillard, would cost about 100 times more than the most basic version. This last type is usually only built by royalty.

A good castle takes plenty of time and money to build.

Time

You also need to prepare for the time it will take. To build a good castle takes several years. The biggest of them can take up to a decade to complete. This is partly because we only build during the warmer months, and not during the planting and harvesting seasons, when labourers will be needed for farm work.

The project begins

Once everything has been agreed and you have your licence to crenellate, you will need to assemble your work team. To build an average-sized castle, you will need around 2500 craftspeople and labourers. You will need:

- carpenters and masons
- quarry workers to provide the stone
- carters to carry it to the site
- miners to dig the huge ditches for the wall foundations
- limeburners to make the **mortar** to cement the blocks together
- plumbers and tilers for the roofing
- blacksmiths to make the nails, locks and portcullises.

Of course, wooden huts will need building to house these workers. Once you have got going with your project, the site will resemble a small, bustling town!

You will be investing a lot of time and money in your castle-building project, and so naturally you will want your castle to last. Yet you should be aware that times change. New weapons will be invented, and castles will have to adapt or die out.

I am writing this in the year 1490, and I cannot know what the situation will be like in twenty or thirty years' time. Today's cannon are more powerful than ever, and increasingly mobile. We master masons will need to adapt, if we can. Otherwise, this could mean the end of the age of castles.

GLOSSARY

besiegers: people who have surrounded somewhere in order to create a siege
blacksmith: person who makes and repairs iron things
breached: made a gap in and broken through (a wall)
budget: plan for spending money
chivalry: a code of good behaviour for knights; honour and consideration
coat of arms: emblem of a noble or knight
dais: platform
garrison: group of soldiers stationed at a castle
insulation: a way of preventing loss of heat
lapis lazuli: a deep-blue stone; can be ground up to make beautiful blue paint
monarch: ruler
mortar: mixture used to bond bricks and stones
Normandy: an area of land, now in northern France
noble: a person of high social rank, like a duchess or a lord
pretender: a person who claims they should be the monarch
royalist: loyal to the monarch
sacked: plundered and destroyed
sieges: military operations in which enemy forces surround a castle and try to force the people inside to surrender
slain: killed
sovereign: ruler
stockade: defensive barrier formed from upright wooden stakes
tapestries: pieces of thick fabric with pictures or designs woven into or embroidered on them
tinder: any dry substance that catches fire easily – usually small twigs
undermining: digging away at a building's foundations until it falls down